PHOTO BY WAGNER INTERNATIONAL PHOTOS

John C. Becher, Charlotte Rae and Paul Vincent in a scene from the New York Television Theater production of "Tour," on the National Educational Television (NET) network.

APPLE PIE

BY TERRENCE McNALLY

THREE ONE ACT PLAYS

★

★

DRAMATISTS
PLAY SERVICE
INC.

For Maurine McElroy

CONTENTS

ABOUT THE AUTHOR

Terrence McNally was raised in Corpus Christi, Texas, then came to New York to attend Columbia University, where he took a B.A. Degree in English in 1960. On graduation he was awarded the Harry Evans Travelling Fellowship for work in creative writing and in 1967 he received a Guggenheim Fellowship.

Mr. McNally was first represented on Broadway in the spring of 1965 with *And Things That Go Bump in the Night,* which starred Eileen Heckart and Robert Drivas at the Royale Theatre. *Apple Pie* was produced with great success by Channel 13 in New York City, and *Tour* was part of *Collision Course* off-Broadway. Recently his work has been seen both on Broadway (*Noon*) and off (*Witness, Sweet Eros* and *Next.*) His plays have also been seen off-off-Broadway and at the Tyrone Guthrie Theatre in Minneapolis, the Mark Taper Forum in Los Angeles, the White Barn Theatre in Westport, Connecticut, and the Berkshire Theatre Festival in Stockbridge, Massachusetts.

Mr. McNally is a member of the Actors Studio and the Playwrights Unit, both in Manhattan, where he lives and works.

TOUR

by

Terrence McNally

TOUR was first performed at the Mark Taper Forum in Los Angeles on October 9, 1967. It was then produced for television on March 14 and 15, 1968, by Channel 13 in New York City. It was most recently presented as a part of "Collision Course" at the Cafe Au Go Go on New York's off-Broadway on May 8, 1968.

CHARACTERS

Mr. Wilson

Mrs. Wilson

Driver

Two Monks

The play's short scenes may be performed as different "postcards": random snapshots of Mr. and Mrs. Wilson abroad. The settings should be non-literal. Simple chairs may be used to form the automobile. Car sounds are suggested to serve as a bridge between each scene.

TOUR

A car. In front, the driver. Mr. and Mrs. Wilson in the back seat. Mrs. Wilson is writing a postcard.

SCENE ONE

MRS. WILSON. Shut up, Woodson.

(Blackout)

SCENE TWO

MRS. WILSON. Shut up, Woodson. (*He looks at her.*) You didn't say anything this time either? (*He slowly shakes his head.*) All right, so I'm on edge! I'll take another nerve pill. My fourth since Rome, thanks to you. At least I think it was Rome. I don't even know what country we're in anymore. And you call this a vacation. It's a Stations of the Cross!
MR. WILSON. Are we still in Italy, driver? (*Driver nods.*)
MRS. WILSON. (*Taking a pill.*) It's so bloody hot and you know how darn sensitive I am to heat. Maybe this just wasn't the summer to travel. Maybe we should have bought that boat instead. I don't know what's right anymore.
MR. WILSON. We're still in Italy.
MRS. WILSON. (*Musing, as she looks out the window.*) Is the sky that red where Chuck sees it, do you think? Is there sky left in Viet Nam? (*She laughs.*) Listen to me!
MR. WILSON. (*As she resumes writing the postcard.*) Poor Cora. (*Pause.*) Dear sweet Cora.
MRS. WILSON. (*Smiling, relaxing.*) That pill works wonders!

(Blackout)

SCENE THREE

MRS. WILSON. Shut up, Woodson.

(*Blackout*)

SCENE FOUR

MR. WILSON. I guess you people get some pretty strange impressions of us Americans. Whew! I read in the *New York Times* . . . you know, giornale . . . where this couple from Shreveport asked their driver how old Moses was when he posed for Michelangelo. I've heard dumb questions before but— (*Looking out the window.*) Cows, Cora! Look at the cows!

MRS. WILSON. They're lying down.

MR. WILSON. They're dead. (*Turning her head away.*) Don't, dear, you'll only upset yourself. (*Back to driver.*) I read something like that and you know, I'm ashamed to say it: "Io sono americano." (*Driver nods.*) Cora and I have our faults but we do know how to travel. We're guests in your country, driver, and we think that's a privilege. So we read up on a place before we get there. We like to mix, meet the people, get off the beaten path . . . that's why we hired you. We drink your water. We eat green vegetables. Why we even stay in your pensiones. (*To Mrs. Wilson.*) In small towns we do! Rome's different. The bathroom was way the hell down the hall in Lucca. Anyway, the point I'm making, puss, so lay off with the sounds, is that we're not his run of the mill, American Express oriented, enterobioform, boiled water, bourbon daiquiris in the Dolomites type tourist. (*The car swerves suddenly.*) Jesus Christ, they can't drive, these Wops!

DRIVER. Stronzo!

MR. WILSON. Still, it's a wonderful race. Even the chauffeurs, so volcanic. (*Looking out the window.*) Look, Cora, peasants! Oh that's a sight to tear your heart out. Better roll up your window.

MRS. WILSON. They're not waving back.

MR. WILSON. Smile at them.

MRS. WILSON. Nothing.

MR. WILSON. The further south we go, you see, life becomes more primitive. Like in the U.S.
MRS. WILSON. Woodson, look, they—!
MR. WILSON. (*Turning her head away.*) Don't look at them, Cora, you'll only upset yourself.

(*Blackout*)

SCENE FIVE

MR. WILSON. Cora!
MRS. WILSON. Well, I did feel sorry for those people. They were so small and dark and underfed compared to us.
MR. WILSON. Sshh! He can hear you, Cora. You'll start something. Italians are called swarthy over here. (*To driver.*) Friends, driver, we are your friends. Amici.
MRS. WILSON. Why would anyone live in such a wretched place? I'm stifling.
MR. WILSON. (*Stopping her from rolling down a window.*) Are you crazy, Cora? Plague! You've got to understand, the further we go, life becomes more primitive. The germs out there are centuries old.
MRS. WILSON. Like in the U.S.

(*Blackout*)

SCENE SIX

MRS. WILSON. (*Reading a postcard.*) "Dear Chuck, greetings from somewhere in Italy."
MR. WILSON. Chuck's our oldest. Viet Nam.
MRS. WILSON. "We are whizzing along, headed for who-knows-where. Daddy wanted to get off the beaten track again. Remember Mexico?"
MR. WILSON. Flash flood. The car broke down.
MRS. WILSON. "Our driver's a nice young man."
MR. WILSON. (*Shushing her.*) He can hear you, Cora!
MRS. WILSON. "Are you well, darling? I think of you in that

jungle, the dangers there, and I worry myself sick. When will this awful trouble be over and you be home with us? Other people's business should be minded by other people, and not by young men like you. Is that too awful of me? I guess women shouldn't even think about things like that. Ha ha ha!"

MR. WILSON. Ha ha ha.

MRS. WILSON. "I bought you a gondalier's shirt in Venice. Blue and white stripes. Cute on you. Your father is well and wants me to ask you: 'Is there sky left in Viet Nam?' Come home soon and safe. Love you. Mom." (*She is crying.*)

MR. WILSON. World peace, driver. Maybe you'll see it in your lifetime. The missus and I won't. Still. And there's the agony, in that one word: "still." (*Pause.*)

MRS. WILSON. (*Sniffling.*) I know we're lost. He made the wrong turn somewhere. I'm sure of it.

MR. WILSON. (*To placate her.*) She thinks we're lost, driver. (*Driver nods.*) We'll be stopping soon, won't we? (*Driver nods.*) This can't be Italy. Still. (*No response from driver.*)

(*Blackout*)

SCENE SEVEN

MRS. WILSON. We are too lost! L-a-o-s.

MR. WILSON. Pussy!

MRS. WILSON. It's like a rain forest, I'm so hot. Just look at that pagoda burning down.

MR. WILSON. It's a pyre, Cora. They're burning victims.

MRS. WILSON. People.

MR. WILSON. Plague victims. Why their plague is as old and inscrutable as Italy itself.

MRS. WILSON. Give me the binoculars.

MR. WILSON. I've told you, honey, the further south we go, life becomes more primitive. They die today, they don't have to die tomorrow. Primitive races are like that. Right, driver? Say, pull over a minute. I want to get a shot of this. Let's see Dot and Hugh's Nassau slides match these. Talk about your fringe benefits. Driver, I said stop! Not go faster!

MRS. WILSON. Use the phrase book on him! (*Craning her neck and looking through the binoculars while he thumbs through the book.*) That column of smoke must be five miles high! So black and oily, not your usual puffs. Smells, too. Viet Nam must be like that.

MR. WILSON. (*Finding the word.*) Fermata! (*The car screeches to a halt.*) Well, never mind now.

MRS. WILSON. We can walk back.

MR. WILSON. We'll see more further on. Go ahead, driver.

MRS. WILSON. Well, I'm getting out for some air. He's starting to . . . (*She pinches her nose.*)

MR. WILSON. Good thinking. (*They get out of the car.*)

MRS. WILSON. Look, natives! (*She waves to them.*)

MR. WILSON. On your P's and Q's now, missy. We're ambassadors.

MRS. WILSON. Where're our suitcases? Your camera and things? My cosmetic bag?

MR. WILSON. In the car.

MRS. WILSON. Well get them, Woodson. He might just drive off. You know what they're like, these people.

MR. WILSON. We *don't* know what they're like. That's why you're right. (*He goes to car but the door is locked.*) Open the door. I forgot . . . I said, open the door. Well open the window then and I'll reach in . . . OPEN THE DOOR. (*Driver doesn't move.*) What do you think you're doing? You can't pull something like this with us. Now look, I told you. We're not your typical tourists. We're not your American boobs.

MRS. WILSON. (*Indicating the approaching people.*) I'll have these men report him to the tourist bureau!

MR. WILSON. What's your name, driver? My wife's going to report you. Goddamn it, we love Italy! Now open this door! (*Two monks appear. They wear orange-brown robes. They are very poor and sickly. They carry wooden begging bowls.*)

MRS. WILSON. Woodson!

FIRST MONK. (*Bowing.*) Prego, signora.

SECOND MONK. (*Pitifully, hands outstretched.*) Pane.

MR. WILSON. No thank you, we . . .

SECOND MONK. Pane.

MR. WILSON. They're begging for bread. (*To monks.*) We do not have any bread.

FIRST MONK. (*Cheerfully bobbing his head.*) Prego!

MR. WILSON. We are locked out of our car. Will you tell our driver to let us in?
FIRST MONK. Prego!
MRS. WILSON. His face, Woodson. That man . . . he has no nose.
FIRST MONK. Prego, signora.
MRS. WILSON. His nose . . . like a leper's . . . eaten away.
MR. WILSON. Now calm yourself, Cora.
MRS. WILSON. Or burned . . . yes! . . . Napalm.
MR. WILSON. Cora, listen to me
MRS. WILSON. I've seen the films.
MR. WILSON. We're in difficult straits, Cora, you've got to keep calm.
MRS. WILSON. I hate jungle.
MR. WILSON. We're on vacation in . . . ! We're just four hours from . . . hotels!
MRS. WILSON. Hate swamp. Smells mud.
MR. WILSON. We have passports, Cora, we know who we are and we're going to pull through. Do I make myself clear?
MRS. WILSON. Napalm Delta. Where's Chuck!
FIRST MONK. Prego, signore!
MR. WILSON. Now listen—!
SECOND MONK. Pane.
MR. WILSON. We are lost. Telefono. Is there a—
SECOND MONK. Pane.
MRS. WILSON. I DON'T HAVE ANY BREAD. TELL HIM, WOODSON!
MR. WILSON. From Rome, we'll send bread from Rome.
FIRST MONK. Prego!
MRS. WILSON. WE ONLY BOMB THE NORTH! BAD PEOPLE!
SECOND MONK. Pane.
MR. WILSON. We'll send money, drugs, anything you want.
MRS. WILSON. WHY DO YOU PEOPLE KEEP BURNING YOURSELVES!
MR. WILSON. Air lift. Cargo planes. Just tell us what you need.
SECOND MONK. Pane!
MR. WILSON. We're strangers. We don't live here.
SECOND MONK. Pane!

MRS. WILSON. LEAVE US ALONE!!! (*Mr. Wilson slaps her. She is calmed.*)
MR. WILSON. (*To monks.*) Now look, buddy, we are tourists. Not your run of the mill tourists, but tourists. We took a wrong turn. We didn't want to come here.
SECOND MONK. Pane!
MR. WILSON. You don't understand! We are Americans, goddamnit! IO SONO AMERICANO!
FIRST MONK. (*A friendly gesture towards them.*) Prego!

(*Blackout*)

SCENE EIGHT

MRS. WILSON. (*They are back in the car, driving along, the three of them again.*) Shut up, Woodson.

(*Blackout*)

SCENE NINE

MR. WILSON. What can we do?

(*Blackout*)

SCENE TEN

MRS. WILSON. Shut up, Woodson.

(*Blackout*)

END OF PLAY

PROPERTY PLOT

Camera

Binoculars

Phrase book

Luggage

Sunglasses (Mrs. Wilson)

Thermos

Pill box (Mrs. Wilson)

Postcard and pen (Mrs. Wilson)

2 begging bowls (Monks)

NEXT

by

Terrence McNally

NEXT was first performed at the White Barn Theatre in Westport, Connecticut, on July 16, 1967. It was then produced on March 14 and 15, 1968, by Channel 13 in New York City. In both productions the role of Marion Cheever was played by James Coco.

CHARACTERS

Marion Cheever

Sgt. Thech

Two Men

Two Attendants

The farcical elements of the play should not be minimized. After all, Marion Cheever is willing to try *anything* to stay out of the Army. His final scenes, of course, are dead serious. Sgt. Thech would be equally at home behind the wheel of a Mack truck as she is behind her desk. She is tough.

NEXT

An examination room. White tables, chairs, small desk, etc. A scales, glass cabinets with instruments, medical charts, wash basin, etc. A man of indeterminate years is being helped from the room by two orderlies. He is babbling, frothing at the mouth, quite hysterical. Sgt. Thech, massive, impassive, bends over the desk writing.

SGT. THECH. Next! (*Marion Cheever enters. He looks apprehensively in the direction they have taken the hysterical man.*)
MARION CHEEVER. One of your Nervous Nellies, hunh? (*False hearty laughter. The sounds of the hysterical man fade away.*) Unh, look. I think we can get this over with rather quickly. There's obviously been some slip up. One of your IBM's . . . I guess you're IBM by now, who isn't . . . punched the wrong little card-ino. I mean, you people tapped the wrong cookie. Uncle Sam wants *you,* mister . . . unh, general! but not this tub o' butter. All you have to do is look at me.
SGT. Strip.
MARION. Sir?
SGT. (*Turning around.*) Sergeant Thech to you, mister.
MARION. You're a woman!
SGT. How's that?
MARION. A lady examining officer! Oh that's a good one. They must be pretty hard up these days.
SGT. Things are tight all over.
MARION. I know, but . . .
SGT. I'm a career officer, mister. So don't knock it. Some people know what their responsibility to their country is. All right, mister, now in the buff!
MARION. Now just a minute. There's been a slip up. Look at me. I'm not draft material.
SGT. No kidding.
MARION. Then let's not waste each other's time.
SGT. You think you know every trick in the book, don't you?
MARION. Sir?

SGT. Sgt. Thech to you, mister.

MARION. Thech, yes. I—

SGT. When it comes time to serve their country, see how they run!

MARION. I know there's a manpower shortage, but surely—

SGT. I'll say there's a manpower shortage. There's a war on, mister, or hadn't you heard? There's a war with guns, a war on poverty, a war for outer space. There's a war on just about anything you can think of. Well I say into the breech.

MARION. Into the—?

SGT. Breech, mister.

MARION. Now look, lady sergeant, colonel, whatever! . . . you can't draft me. Some young punk with my name is meant to be here.

SGT. They're taking older men.

MARION. How old exactly?

SGT. It's inching up, all the time. Maybe you're next. And if you're not stripped in thirty seconds I'll have you watching radar up on some tundra before you know what's hit you.

MARION. But you're a woman.

SGT. How's that?

MARION. I am a male. We can't—

SGT. Unsex yourself.

MARION. Sir?

SGT. Unsex yourself.

MARION. Unsex . . .?

SGT. Strip!

MARION. (*Unbuttoning his shirt.*) I've heard of crazy mixups but this . . .

SGT. (*At desk, filling out forms.*) Name.

MARION. Marion Cheever.

SGT. "O-n"?

MARION. What?

SGT. Do you spell Marion with an "o-n"?

MARION. Well of course I do!

SGT. Don't snip, Cheever.

MARION. I'm not—

SGT. Age.

MARION. Thirty—forty-eight!

SGT. Sex.

MARION. Did you put that down? I'm forty-eight years old. Oh hell, why lie? I'm over fifty. I'm practically dead.
SGT. Sex.
MARION. What are all those 18-year-old punks doing on the street? Draft them.
SGT. Sex.
MARION. What do you think, goddamnit!
SGT. I'm a woman, Cheever. So can that mouth.
MARION. (*Imitating Sgt.*) How's that?
SGT. (*Dense.*) What?
MARION. Never mind.
SGT. Occupation?
MARION. Dancer.
SGT. Toe or tap?
MARION. I'm an office worker! White collar. Wanna see?
SGT. I'll ask the questions, Cheever. Marital status.
MARION. I'll refuse to go you understand. You're just wasting your time.
SGT. Marital status.
MARION. I'll picket the White House. I'll . . . I'll . . . !
SGT. Marital status.
MARION. Single!
SGT. Figures.
MARION. Single now. Divorced I guess is what I'm supposed to say.
SGT. How many times?
MARION. Is it that common?
SGT. How many times?
MARION. Twice. You? No, you've probably just been annulled.
SGT. Number of dependents.
MARION. Three girls.
SGT. Sex.
MARION. I said three girls!
SGT. Ages.
MARION. Fourteen, twelve and two. (*Short pause.*) Two with my first wife and one with my second!
SGT. So I gathered! Now get that shirt off.
MARION. (*Obeying.*) I'm going to write somebody a letter about this. It's humiliating, that's what it is.
SGT. Suck that gut in, Cheever.

MARION. (*Gasping for air.*) I was! All right, look at me. Now are you satisfied? I'm not ashamed. Take it all in. Look, look at that inner tube. I am what you call a fat man. Don't do that! (*She has applied a stethoscope to his bare chest.*)
SGT. (*After listening a while.*) You're not cooperating, Cheever. Now breathe! In. Out. In. Out. In. Out. Out. Out. Out. (*Writes something down.*) Unh-hunh!
MARION. (*Anxiously.*) What does that mean? It's irregular, right? Boom-boom-BOOM-boom-boom-boom-boom-boom-BOOM-BOOM! No, wait, it's too faint. You could scarcely hear it.
SGT. (*With a tongue depressor.*) Open.
MARION. And you heard that death rattle—? Gahhhhhhh! (*She has the tongue depressor halfway down his throat.*)
SGT. (*Writing it down.*) Garlic, Cheever?
MARION. Oh I have terrible breath, sergeant. Nobody likes to come near me. And the spots on my tongue. Be sure you note the spots on my tongue. They could be a sign of . . . anything!
SGT. . . .
MARION. What? What did you say?
SGT. Your hearing's perfect.
MARION. I will not be railroaded!
SGT. Read that chart.
MARION. What chart? I don't see any chart.
SGT. There!
MARION. I couldn't possibly make that out.
SGT. The third line.
MARION. Nothing.
SGT. The second.
MARION. Would you believe this, but it's even fuzzier?
SGT. Try the top line, Cheever.
MARION. "A."
SGT. Excellent.
MARION. Now wait a minute! It's a "Z." I said it was an "A." Now I failed that test. You give me credit for failing.
SGT. Failure is relative in *any* case, Cheever, but especially in yours. If Uncle Sam wants you, private, Uncle Sam gets you.
MARION. Private?
SGT. Run.
MARION. You called me private!

SGT. Get those knees going, Cheever. Up and down. Up and down.

MARION. (*Running in place.*) You've got me inducted already when I haven't even been given a full opportuntiy to fail yet.

SGT. Hup! Hup!

MARION. I've heard of shanghaiing but this little episode is really a lulu. It's white slavery if you think I'm passing this test. Out and out kidnapping. I simply won't go. What do they want with me anyway? I'm on the verge of my Big Break. Do you know what that means to a civilian? I've sweated out that lousy job at that lousy office for twenty years and they are going to promote me next month. I'm not going into any army, sergeant, war or peace!

SGT. Shut up, Cheever.

MARION. Sure I'll shut up because next I'm going to have a heart attack right on your floor. You're driving me to it. Oh and then there'll be hell to pay. Go ahead. Make me have a heart attack. See if I care. I'm not going into any army. You sweat, you slave, you're up to here in alimony and time payments and they think you'll let them draft you. Sergeant, you are looking at a man on the verge of his Big Breakdown. I mean Breakthrough. I will not go!

SGT. Stop.

MARION. Look how I'm sweating. Now listen to my heart, I dare you. Oh. Oh. I feel faint.

SGT. Drop your pants.

MARION. What?

SGT. You heard me.

MARION. Drop my pants? No. That I flatly refuse.

SGT. You are a candidate for national service, Cheever. I am your examining officer and I am ordering you to drop your pants.

MARION. I'm not wearing any shorts.

SGT. Aha! (*She writes something down.*)

MARION. (*Trying to see over her shoulder.*) There! You see? There is something wrong with me. Men who don't wear shorts are capable of anything. Only the other day, that man who went berserk and murdered his mother-in-law, he wasn't wearing shorts! (*Sergeant's gaze is granite.*) Drop my pants.

SGT. Cough.

MARION. Oh really!

SGT. Cough.
MARION. Cough.
SGT. Again.
MARION. Cough.
SGT. Again.
MARION. How many hernias are you checking for? Two's about average, you know. Cough.
SGT. Well done, Cheever. Now sit.
MARION. You're a real master sergeant, you are. You and Pegeen ought to team up. She was my first wife.
SGT. Sit.
MARION. Talk about your lady wrestlers and roller derby queens! Next to her, they were Snow White.
SGT. Cross your legs.
MARION. (*While she taps with a mallet, determined to fail this test, too.*) Oh but I foxed her. Just when she thought she had me where she wanted me, I sprang the divorce on her.
SGT. Tap.
MARION. "On what grounds, may I ask?" she growled . . . fat hands on her fat hips . . . "Dutch Cleanser" I used to call her. "On exactly what grounds?"
SGT. Tap!
MARION. "Mental cruelty" I smiled and oh does that answer ever throw the ladies for a loop! She begged I change it to adultery but I held firm. You should have seen the look on that judge's face in Juarez when I dropped that little bombshell. "Mental"—
SGT. Tap!
MARION. (*Can't hold it back any longer.*) Aaaahh!
SGT. All right, Cheever. The examination is over.
MARION. Over? OVER! What about the rest of me? My feet. They're flat, they're covered with corns. My hemorrhoid condition. X-rays, the curve of my spine!
SGT. Get your pants on.
MARION. I failed, didn't I? You're not going to accept me?
SGT. You'll hear in the mail.
MARION. You haven't really looked at me! My hair's falling out in bushels. (*He tears his hair.*) There. See all those strands? Coming out at the roots, they are! (*On scales.*) Come here. Write this down. I weigh close to three hundred pounds. (*Gets*

off.) I've got dandruff, athlete's foot. You've got to believe me, sergeant, I'm a dying man!

SGT. The army is large, Cheever. There's a niche here for nearly everyone.

MARION. Niches are small things and I am a very large person.

SGT. Stop whimpering, Cheever. Pull yourself together. Be a man. Set an example for me.

MARION. All right, have it your way. But I demand further testing! My IQ, my medical history, my psychological make-up. Everything. The works!

SGT. You're sure, Cheever?

MARION. I'm demanding it!

SGT. You're sure you're sure?

MARION. Of course I'm sure I'm sure! (*Sergeant writes something down.*) What was that? What did that mark mean?

SGT. I have twelve apples.

MARION. Hunh?

SGT. I have twelve apples. You have twelve apples. (*Marion is looking for the apples.*) Together we have . . .

MARION. (*Still distracted.*) Twenty-four apples. NO! wait, that's wrong. How could I be so stupid? (*Counting on fingers.*) It's nineteen. Of course it's nineteen. If you have twelve apples and I have twelve apples, together we have nineteen apples. Whew! You really threw me a curve with that question. Twenty-four!

SGT. The Viennese waltz . . .

MARION. (*Always trying to see what Sergeant has written down.*) Nineteen my answer was.

SGT. (*First a glare, then continuing.*) The Viennese Waltz is associated with which of the following cities? You have a multiple choice here. Chicago or Vienna?

MARION. Chicago, definitely Chicago. (*Humming.*) "Chicago, Chicago. . . ."

SGT. This one's abstract logic, Cheever. A man jumps off the Empire State Building. (A) he falls to the ground or (B) he hovers.

MARION. B! He hovers . . . he just floats up there, treading air.

SGT. (*Turning to a new page.*) Chicken pox.

MARION. That was the IQ test? We're into medical history already?
SGT. Chicken pox.
MARION. Twice a year.
SGT. Mumps?
MARION. (*Puffing out his cheeks.*) Mmmmmmm.
SGT. Hay fever?
MARION. Atchoo!
SGT. Venereal disease.
MARION. I'm riddled with it. The health department's got a $500 reward out for me.
SGT. Epilepsy.
MARION. (*Flipping out of the chair.*) Gngngngngngngngngn!
SGT. (*Coolly looking at him on the floor.*) Insanity in the family.
MARION. (*Eating the rug.*) We're all nuts. Presidential assassins, rapists, necro-something-or-acs!
SGT. (*Sighs, turns to a new page.*) Have you ever or are you now . . .
MARION. You can't have finished with the medical history too!
SGT. . . . indulged and/or indulging in homosexual activities?
MARION. (*Seizing a golden opportunity.*) Oh all the time. I'm a terrible swish, sergeant. I mean it's all I do, just swish! That was such a lie about the wives and all. I mean, who'd want one? Oh I stay home weekends with Sammy . . . he's my roomie; we're practically married . . . and we paint ourselves up, do each other's hair, put on dresses. Oh I tell you, it's a lark! the things we girls do!
SGT. (*A dramatic gesture; pulling down a rolled up poster of a naked man.*) Look at that chart.
MARION. I'm going to faint! Now I am really quite beside myself. That is the most gorgeous—
SGT. And this. (*Chart of naked woman.*)
MARION. Oh. Oh. Take it away. Disgusting. Horrible. I can't stand to look even. No what-do-you-call-it. Those big things hanging down. Oh please, sergeant, take it away.
SGT. Any history of bed-wetting, private?
MARION. (*Not hearing, too lost in his performance.*) All right, so I'm queer, put it in writing. I'm one of your pansies, sergeant, one of your twilight men. Go ahead, get it over with, stamp me

4-F, and then I'll just flounce out of here and never bother you people again. (*His head is hanging low.*)

SGT. About your bed-wetting, Cheever.

MARION. Now look, lady, I just told you I was queer! You can't draft queers!

SGT. Don't fret, Cheever. They've inaugurated special units for men like you.

MARION. Special units? What do you mean, special units?

SGT. Use your imagination, Cheever.

MARION. I am and I don't like what I'm seeing! I hate queers. I practically did my wives' hair myself I hate them so much. I don't even use after-shave. And deodorants only in July and August. I love women, sergeant! That's my real problem. I'm a satyr. You know, those goat-men with the little horns who went around raping everything in sight. I mean they're like a sickness with me, women are. I see one and—you! You sergeant! I haven't seen a body like yours in . . . ever! The . . . the . . . (*Desperately trying to find something to say about her.*) . . . the bulk of your calves rising like granite tusks out of your shoes.

SGT. Shoes. Aha! (*Writes something down.*)

MARION. You've found me out, I've revealed myself and it's worse than anything! Oh my shoe fetish, sergeant! I can't stop myself. I've been arrested twice for breaking shoe shop windows just because I couldn't keep from throwing myself into all that ladies leather! Your shoes, sergeant. Kiss me.

SGT. Your bed-wetting, Cheever.

MARION. I pee all over the place. Even my top sheet's rubber. My pajamas. Everything's rubber!

SGT. Did you have a normal relation with your mother?

MARION. Sure, after I killed father and we went off to Niagara Falls everything was perfect.

SGT. Arc you now or have you ever been . . .

MARION. (*Rapturous interruption.*) Yes! Yes!

SGT. . . . a member of the Communist party!

MARION. I welcomed a Viet Cong victory! I went on pilgrimages to Lenin's tomb. I'm a spy. I'm a dove. Peace marches, protest rallies. Give me a draft card, I'll burn it. See, see! In effigy I trample the American flag. Yes! oh God yes, I am an enemy of the state! (*Pause, he has exhausted himself.*)

SGT. Only one more question, private.

MARION. Private? Now you stop calling me that. I'm not done in here. I want more testing. You're not convinced, I can tell by that look on your face. I'm not leaving until I get a better verdict!

SGT. What is your responsibility to your country, private?

MARION. What is my re—? to my coun—?

SGT. (*Nodding.*) What is your responsibility to your country?

MARION. What about its responsibility to me? I haven't had a straight answer since I walked in here. You can't just take a man out of civilian life and plop him into the army. I pay my taxes. I serve my jury duty. I buy American. Now tell me this suit looks like it was made in Japan. All right, so there's a war on. I didn't start it. Look, I'm on the verge of my Big Breakthrough. Just leave me alone. Oh all right, it's an ugly war. Young men are being killed. I feel sorry for them. But not me. They can't take me.

SGT. What is your responsibility to your—?

MARION. I'm not walking into any one of your traps, sergeant. No sir, you won't catch me playing one of your intellectuals. You want to know about me? All right, I'll tell you. I've never been arrested, I go to church, . . . well, most of the time, I've never killed anyone. I don't make trouble. Period. The End.

SGT. What is your responsibility to—?

MARION. Stop asking me that question! All I want to know is am I being taken or not?

SGT. What is your responsibility—?

MARION. I love this country! All right? Other than air pollution, it's terrific. It's a ginger-peachy place to be from! (*Singing.*)

"God bless America
Land that I love."

SGT. What is your—?

MARION. Look, lady, I just want to get ahead in the world. I've got this job and I've got car payments and alimony. I just want my kids to have the best even if their mothers are going to be the ruin of them. I hope they clean up crime in the streets, give the Negroes whatever the hell it is they want, I hope old people get Cadillacs. I hope all the best for this country.

SGT. What is—?

MARION. Come on! I'm an ordinary Joe. What is it with you? You want me to give you a big answer? All right, here's my big answer. My responsibility to my country is to keep my nose clean. Yeah! And I do that, my country leaves me alone. War's for young men. Hell, those kids enjoy shooting those Commies up. All right, so maybe they are a threat. I'll be dead by the time anything big happens, so leave me out of it. I just want to go along my way and die. And when I go, I'm paying for my own funeral. Those slobs on relief, can they say that?

SGT. What—?

MARION. I HAVE NO RESPONSIBILITY TO MY COUNTRY. I mean . . . well maybe I don't. I've been married twice . . . you think it's fun, my age, going home alone at night! Who looks at men like me after a while? What do my kids think of me? Goddamnit, I miss them. What does my country care about that? Know what they call me at the office? Fatso. Yeah, that hurts, but I'm on the verge of a Big Breakdown and I'm gonna laugh at them. They killed the president, what kind of lousy country does that happen in? I served in the last war and what did that get me? Nothing. A letter saying I did good. How was my country responsible to me? And anyway, what *is* this country, lady? You tell me, because you know what? I don't have much to do with it. Give me something I can put my finger on and tell me that's my country. A bunch of long faces in Washington, a couple of monuments, killing people everywhere. I can't put my finger on any of that. I'm going to get older and fatter and someday I'm going to die. Don't ask me what my responsibility is. I got car payments due and I don't know where the money is coming from. My Big Breakdown? A lousy twenty bucks raise. Big deal, yeah! When I was a kid I had polio. I limped till I was twelve. What do I have now? Anything better? I'm at war with the whole system if anybody cared to listen. I don't know where I'm at. Yesterday they knifed a man two blocks from where I live. He didn't have a cigarette. That's a reason to kill someone? Maybe it is in my country. I mean what's the purpose of doing a thing like that? The purpose! Ask me that. Ask me our national purpose and I'll tell you I don't know what the hell is happening. Don't tell me about responsibility until I know your purpose. (*The two attendants have come into the room.*) Where are we headed? Down, that's where I think. This boat is sinking and I want off. You see those teen-age girls with their skirts up to here strutting around with their hair all piled up and thinking mellow yellow and driving a man crazy? And those men all like fags with that hair and those pants and you ask me what my Big Breakdown to my country is? The Roman Empire collapsed the way we are. I mean Peking is breathing down my neck and I'm strapped with a hot red Mustang and I can hardly fit behind the wheel of and you ask me what my responsibility to a Breakdown is? I'll tell you. I'll tell you, mister. Snow's falling only it ain't snow, it's some goddamn chemical they're putting in the sky and when I shut my eyes now I see faces all garbled up and women with their hair off and I DON'T WANT TO GO and I'm sick of watching television and LEAVE ME ALONE and I'm paying taxes and WHERE AM I AT and I want to kill Avon Calling and I DON'T KNOW WHAT'S RIGHT and the president is dead and I AM SINKING and when I was little nobody asked me questions and I WANT I DON'T KNOW WHAT I WANT and . . . and . . . and . . . (*The two attendants are helping him from the room.*)

SGT. (*At the desk, massive, impassive.*) Next. (*Marion's voice is fading. A man of indeterminate years has appeared at the door.*) Name.

CURTAIN—END OF PLAY

PROPERTY PLOT

Desk, with pen, papers, etc.

Chairs

American Flag

Recruiting poster

Stethoscope

Tongue depressor

Eye chart

Scales

Anatomy charts

Mallet

NEXT

by

Terrence McNally

(Revised version, as presented off-Broadway in New York City.)

For
James Coco

The revised script of NEXT which follows was first presented by the Theatre-In-Progress Workshop of the Berkshire Theatre Festival on August 29, 1968, at the Barn, Stockbridge, Massachusetts, with the following cast:

MARION CHEEVER	JAMES COCO
SGT. THECH	ELAINE SHORE

Directed by Elaine May

This version was then presented by Lyn Austin on February 10, 1969, at the Greenwich News Playhouse, New York City, with the following cast:

MARION CHEEVER	JAMES COCO
SGT. THECH	ELAINE SHORE

Directed by Elaine May

NEXT

The scene opens in an examination room decorated in neutral colors, anonymous-looking. At L. *there is an examination table, a scale and a cabinet filled with medical equipment. At* R. *there is a desk and two chairs. The only bright color in the room is the American flag, at* C.
As the curtain rises, the room is empty.

SGT. THECH. (*Offstage.*) Next! (*Marion Cheever enters. He is a fat man in his late forties and he is nattily dressed. He carries a brief case.*)
MARION. Hello? I'm next! (*He looks around, puts down his brief case, takes out a cigarette case, lights one up, sits in front of the desk and waits somewhat impatiently.*)
SGT. THECH. (*Entering.*) No smoking.
MARION. (*Rising.*) Good morning. Good morning! (*Briskly.*) Well! I think we can get this over with rather quickly.
SGT. THECH. No smoking.
MARION. (*Snuffing out his cigarette.*) I'm sorry. Filthy habit. (*He's put his hat on her desk. Sgt. Thech hands it back to him.*) Oh my hat! I'm sorry! (*He looks for a place to put it. There is none, so he puts it on the floor.*)
SGT. THECH. (*Already busy at her desk with papers and forms.*) Your card and bottle, please.
MARION. (*Rummaging in his brief case.*) As I was starting to say, I think we can get this over with rather quickly. There's obviously been a mistake. (*He laughs.*) I mean I—
SGT. THECH. The government does not make mistakes. If your country has called you it has its reasons. May I have your card and bottle, please?
MARION. (*Still going through his brief case.*) I thought to myself, "My God! They can't mean me."
SGT. THECH. That's it.
MARION. Is that it? (*Hands her the card. She begins to type.*) I thought to myself there must be someone else in my building with

the same name because why else would I get a card to come down here?

SGT. THECH. Is your name Marion Cheever?

MARION. Yes, it is. But you know I just had a fortieth birthday and I thought to myself nobody sends a card like this to a man like me.

SGT. THECH. They're taking older men.

MARION. How old exactly?

SGT. THECH. It's inching up all the time. May I have your bottle, please?

MARION. (*Looking in brief case.*) Inching up all the time, is it? The bottle, yes, here it is! (*He hands her his urine specimen.*)

SGT. THECH. Strip.

MARION. I didn't know that . . . the inching up all the time.

SGT. THECH. Remove all articles of clothing including your shoes and socks.

MARION. Who are you?

SGT. THECH. Your examining officer, Sgt. Thech. And by the authority vested in me by this government, I order you to strip.

MARION. A lady examining officer! Oh that's funny! They must be pretty hard up these days.

SGT. THECH. And if you have not begun to strip in the next ten seconds I will complete these forms without further examination and report you to the board of examiners as fit for duty.

MARION. (*As if coming out of a trance.*) Oh my God, I'm sorry. I didn't hear one word you said. I don't know what I was thinking of. What did you say? That if I hadn't—

SGT. THECH. Begun to strip in the next ten seconds . . .

MARION. You will complete those forms . . .

SGT. THECH. Without further examination . . .

MARION. And report me to the board of examiners? . . .

SGT. THECH. As fit for duty.

MARION. (*Biting his lip.*) Do you think that's fair?

SGT. THECH. Would you prefer not to strip?

MARION. Indeed I would!

SGT. THECH. Very well, then I will stamp these forms—

MARION. No, don't do that!

SGT. THECH. Then you have ten seconds. (*Timing him.*) One one-thousand, two one-thousand . . .

MARION. I'm going to strip! (*While Sgt. Thech counts.*) I'm going to let you do it because not only am I over forty, I am not a healthy over forty and—

SGT. THECH. Seven one-thousand.

MARION. (*To make her stop.*) Where do I go?

SGT. THECH. (*Points to* C.) Right over there.

MARION. Right over there. Well! Everybody else is doing it, why not?

SGT. THECH. (*Filling out a questionnaire.*) Your name.

MARION. Do you have a little hanger?

SGT. THECH. Use the stool. Your name.

MARION. Cheever. Marion Cheever.

SGT. THECH. Do you spell Marion with an *o*?

MARION. I do, yes.

SGT. THECH. Age.

MARION. Forty . . . eight! Forty-eight.

SGT. THECH. Sex.

MARION. Did you put that down? I'm forty-eight years old.

SGT. THECH. Sex.

MARION. Well what do you think I am?

SGT. THECH. Color of hair.

MARION. Brown. Black. Blackish brown.

SGT. THECH. Eyes.

MARION. Two.

SGT. THECH. Color of eyes . . .

MARION. I'm sorry! Blue. Blue-green. Aqua.

SGT. THECH. Occupation.

MARION. (*Still apologizing for the eyes.*) You rattled me.

SGT. THECH. Occupation.

MARION. I don't know what's the matter with me.

SGT. THECH. Your occupation, Mr. Cheever.

MARION. I'm a dancer.

SGT. THECH. Toe or tap?

MARION. Oh really! Toe or tap! I'm the assistant manager of the Fine Arts Theatre, 58th Street and Park Avenue. You've probably heard of us. Toe or tap! I was funning!

SGT. THECH. How long.

MARION. Is what?

SGT. THECH. How long have you been the assistant manager of the Fine Arts Theatre?

MARION. I'm sorry. How long have I been assistant manager of the Fine Arts Theatre? About twelve years. (*He has removed his shirt by now. His undershirt is torn and dirty. He's trying to find something to hide behind.*)
SGT. THECH. Marital status.
MARION. (*Eying the American flag.*) Single. Single now. Divorced I guess is what I'm supposed to say. (*He will use the flag to cover himself as he continues to strip. Sgt. Thech doesn't see all this, as he is behind her and she is busy typing in the questionnaire.*)
SGT. THECH. How many times.
MARION. Twice.
SGT. THECH. Number of dependents.
MARION. Three girls.
SGT. THECH. Sex.
MARION. I said three girls!
SGT. THECH. Ages.
MARION. Fourteen, twelve and two. Two with my first wife and one with my second.
SGT. THECH. Did you finish grammar school?
MARION. I certainly did.
SGT. THECH. High school.
MARION. You bet.
SGT. THECH. College.
MARION. No, I never got to college. I meant to but I never—
SGT. THECH. Do you belong to a church?
MARION. I just never got there. You know what I mean?
SGT. THECH. Do you belong to a church?
MARION. Oh yes!
SGT. THECH. Which denomination.
MARION. The Sacred Heart of Jesus.
SGT. THECH. Which denomination.
MARION. Roman Catholic. What do you think with a name like that? It's a temple?
SGT. THECH. Do you attend church?
MARION. You bet.
SGT. THECH. Regularly or occasionally.
MARION. Yes, unh-hunh, unh-hunh!
SGT. THECH. Regularly or occasionally.
MARION. Yes, regularly on occasion.

SGT. THECH. Is your father living or deceased.
MARION. Living.
SGT. THECH. His age.
MARION. Seventy-two.
SGT. THECH. Is your mother living or deceased.
MARION. Deceased.
SGT. THECH. Age of death.
MARION. Thirty-one.
SGT. THECH. Cause of death.
MARION. Natural causes.
SGT. THECH. Be specific.
MARION. Heart.
SGT. THECH. Any brothers.
MARION. Yes.
SGT. THECH. How many.
MARION. One. He's alive.
SGT. THECH. Sisters.
MARION. Two. They're both alive. Both living.
SGT. THECH. Do you live alone?
MARION. At the present time I do. I get a lot of compony of course, but unh, officially, for the record, I live alone.
SGT. THECH. Do you own your own home?
MARION. No. It's a . . . you know . . . residential hotel for . . . unh . . . men. Single men. (*Marion has undressed now and is sitting on a low stool. The flag is draped across him.*)
SGT. THECH. (*Turning to a new page.*) Measles.
MARION. What?
SGT. THECH. Have you ever had the measles?
MARION. Oh measles! No, no I haven't.
SGT. THECH. Chicken pox.
MARION. No, I never had chicken pox.
SGT. THECH. Whooping cough.
MARION. I think it *might* have been. I was coughing an awful lot and I was very sick.
SGT. THECH. Yes or no.
MARION. No. It wasn't *exactly* whooping cough but—
SGT. THECH. Rheumatic fever.
MARION. (*Thinking hard.*) Unh! Did I have rheumatic fever? Is that what it was? No, no I don't think so.
SGT. THECH. Mumps.

MARION. (*Jumping at this.*) Yes! Yes, yes, yes! Now just a minute on the mumps.
SGT. THECH. Tuberculosis.
MARION. They weren't your ordinary mumps.
SGT. THECH. Jaundice.
MARION. Will you please let me tell you about my mumps. I was in bed for months. I practically had last rites!
SGT. THECH. Venereal disease.
MARION. I don't think you realize how serious my mumps were.
SGT. THECH. Venereal disease.
MARION. Not yet! I just wish you'd let me tell you about my mumps!
SGT. THECH. Allergies.
MARION. What about allergies?
SGT. THECH. Are you allergic to anything?
MARION. Yes, yes, as a matter of fact I am.
SGT. THECH. Go on, explain.
MARION. I know this sounds silly but I'm allergic to peach fuzz. I swell up like a balloon.
SGT. THECH. Anything else.
MARION. No, but I can't even go *near* a fruit stand. All I have to do is look at a peach and—
SGT. THECH. Any history of epilepsy.
MARION. Me and peach fuzz is no joke!
SGT. THECH. Have you a family history of diabetes?
MARION. Diabetes? Well why not. Somebody must have had it.
SGT. THECH. Heart attacks.
MARION. I told you about that.
SGT. THECH. Cancer.
MARION. Bite your tongue!
SGT. THECH. Nervous or mental disorders.
MARION. I'm a nervous wreck!
SGT. THECH. Do you smoke?
MARION. You saw me. Remember? When you came in here, the first thing you said—
SGT. THECH. How much?
MARION. Three packs a day. Twenty cigarettes to a pack, that's sixty cigarettes. That's a lot of smoking.
SGT. THECH. Do you drink.
MARION. That, too, oh yes!

SGT. THECH. How much.

MARION. Whenever I smoke. Smoking makes me want to drink and drinking makes me want to smoke. It's a vicious circle.

SGT. THECH. Do you take any drugs?

MARION. Anything! Give it to me and I'll take it.

SGT. THECH. Name the drugs.

MARION. Aspirins and bromo seltzers for the hangovers, Nikoban for the smoking. And Miltown! I take lots of Miltown.

SGT. THECH. For what purpose.

MARION. Because I am a nervous wreck. For what purpose!

SGT. THECH. All right, Mr. Cheever, on the scale now, please. (*She turns and sees him draped in the American flag.*) Drop that flag.

MARION. I was just admiring it! I have one just like it at home. (*Sgt. Thech returns the flag to its proper place. Marion all the while walks along with it, unwilling to give up its protection.*) The same colors, the same shape. It's amazing how similar they are! (*Sgt. Thech is pulling the flag away from him.*) Then could I have a little robe or something? I mean I don't know if it's of any interest to you but I'm right on the verge of another bad cold. (*Sgt. Thech hands him a sheet.*) Thank you. Thank you. (*Sgt. Thech salutes the flag, then makes ready to examine Marion.*) I'm going to write somebody a letter about this.

SGT. THECH. On the scale.

MARION. (*Wrapping the sheet around himself.*) I'll refuse to go, you know. You're just wasting your time. I hope you understand.

SGT. THECH. On the scale, Mr. Cheever. (*Marion gets on the scale and plays with the weights.*)

MARION. You know something? It's wrong. At least ten pounds off. Easily that.

SGT. THECH. Don't tamper. (*She is washing her hands.*)

MARION. What are you going to do? Operate? (*Sgt. Thech comes to the scale and weighs him. Next, she makes ready to measure him. When she raises up the measuring pole, Marion starts and backs off the scale.*) Would you warn someone before you do that? You know you could put someone's eye out with that thing.

SGT. THECH. Step back onto the scale. (*Marion gets back onto scale while Sgt. Thech measures him. When she swings the pole back into place Marion jumps off again.*)

MARION. You missed me by *that* much!
SGT. THECH. (*At the examining table.*) Sit at the edge of the table.
MARION. (*Under his breath.*) I hate this whole day! It's goddamn humiliating, that's what it is. Calling a man in here and—
SGT. THECH. On the table, Mr. Cheever.
MARION. (*Trying a new approach.*) I'm sorry I'm not cooperating. You have your job to do and I'll try to help in every way I can.
SGT. THECH. (*At his back, listening with a stethoscope.*) Breathe. In, out. In, out.
MARION. In, out. See when you ask me how simple it is? (*Sgt. Thech's stethoscope is at his chest now. Marion is very ticklish.*) Don't do that! (*He laughs while Sgt. Thech listens to his heart.*)
SGT. THECH. Unh-hunh!
MARION. What did that mean? "Unh-hunh?" You heard something you didn't like?
SGT. THECH. Open. (*She has a tongue depressor down his throat.*)
MARION. Just ask me and I'll open! You don't have to lunge at me like that! (*Sgt. Thech checks his eyes with a light.*) It's on, it's on! (*Sgt. Thech looks into his ears with a light.*) I hate this. I hate it a lot. (*While Sgt. Thech checks his ears.*) When you were examining my heart, did you hear something I should know about? It wasn't very subtle, going "unh-hunh" like that. It's my ticker, so if there's anything wrong I'd like to know about it. (*Sgt. Thech has crossed the room. She turns to face him and speaks very softly. We just see her lips moving.*) What? What did you say?
SGT. THECH. Your hearing is perfect.
MARION. Now just a minute. I will not be railroaded.
SGT. THECH. (*Holding up an eye chart.*) Read this chart.
MARION. All of it?
SGT. THECH. The third line.
MARION. (*Running all the letters together.*) TOZDY!
SGT. THECH. The second line.
MARION. The second line's a little fuzzy.
SGT. THECH. Try the top line, Mr. Cheever.
MARION. (*With much squinting.*) The top line's a real problem. Let's see . . . it's a . . . no . . . Z!

SGT. THECH. Excellent.
MARION. Now just a minute. It's an Ɛ. I said it was a Z. Now I failed that test. You give me credit for failing.
SGT. THECH. Failure is relative in any case, private.
MARION. Private?
SGT. THECH. (*Back at the examining table.*) Lie down.
MARION. You called me private.
SGT. THECH. Lie down.
MARION. You've got me inducted already when I haven't even been given a full opportunity to fail yet.
SGT. THECH. This is your opportunity, Mr. Cheever, don't pass it up. (*Timing him until he obeys.*) One one-thousand, two one-thousand. . . .
MARION. (*Getting onto the table.*) All right, I'm lying! Just stop all that counting. (*Sgt. Thech begins to take his blood pressure.*) I've heard of shanghaiing but this little episode is really a lulu. It's white slavery if you think I'm passing this test. Out and out kid-napping. I simply won't go. You can't just take a man out of civilian life and plop him into the army. So there's a war on, I didn't start it. (*Lifts his head up a moment.*) I think you'll find I have a labile blood pressure. It can rocket at a moment's notice.
SGT. THECH. Keep your head down.
MARION. What do they want with me anyway? I'm on the verge of my big break. Do you know what that means to a civilian? I've stood in the back of that lousy theatre for eleven years and they are going to promote me next winter. I am going to be *the* manager at quite a substantial raise in salary, thank you. Unh-hunh, sergeant, I'm not going into any army, war or peace!
SGT. THECH. (*While she makes ready to take a blood sample.*) I want you to close your eyes and count to ten slowly and then touch the tip of your nose with your left index finger.
MARION. Oh, all right, that sounds easy. I don't mind this part at all. One, two, three, four . . . this is very restful . . . five, six— (*Suddenly sitting up.*) Wait! Wait, wait, wait, wait, wait! I saw it. (*Sgt. Thech is holding a syringe.*) I hate needles. I'm not afraid of them, I just don't like them.
SGT. THECH. Shall I complete the forms, Mr. Cheever, or will you let me continue with the examination?
MARION. I know you must do your job, but please be very careful. I have very small veins. Don't be nervous.

SGT. THECH. Lie down.

MARION. You have all the time in the world. And no air bubbles! (*Sgt. Thech is drawing blood.*) Oh my God! I'm going to have a heart attack right on this table. (*Sgt. Thech finishes, empties his blood from the syringe into a test tube.*) I'm bleeding. Look at this, I'm bleeding. (*Sgt. Thech's hands go under the sheet as she checks his spleen, liver, kidney, etc.*) Just tell me what it is you're looking for and I'll tell you where it's at!

SGT. THECH. In.

MARION. In!

SGT. THECH. Out.

MARION. It's out!

SGT. THECH. In.

MARION. In! In! Oh my God, oh!

SGT. THECH. On your feet.

MARION. On my feet! Bleed someone to death and tell him on his feet. Sure, why not? Here I go, sergeant, on my feet!

SGT. THECH. Drop your shorts.

MARION. What?

SGT. THECH. You heard me. (*Timing him.*) One one-thousand, two one-thousand . . .

MARION. Drop my shorts? Oh no, sergeant, that I flatly refuse.

SGT. THECH. You are a candidate for national service. I am your examining officer and I am ordering you to drop your shorts.

MARION. (*While Sgt. Thech counts.*) Now wait just a minute. Let me explain something. I'm not wearing shorts. I have this . . . well, *problem* . . . and I have to wear this . . . well sort of a *girdle* and—

SGT. THECH. Drop your girdle.

MARION. (*As Sgt. Thech is nearing the count of ten.*) Yes! Yes, of course, I'll drop it. I just thought I should explain about my back problem and the abdominal muscles. I thought you'd want to know about them. (*Marion has worked off the girdle. It drops to the floor. Sgt. Thech is approaching him.*) It's off! I swear to God it's off! (*Sgt. Thech has her hand under sheet and at his groin.*)

SGT. THECH. Turn your head and cough.

MARION. Oh really!

SGT. THECH. Cough.

MARION. Cough!

SGT. THECH. Again.

MARION. Cough!
SGT. THECH. Again.
MARION. How many hernias are you checking for? Two's about average, you know. Cough!
SGT. THECH. Well done, Cheever. Now sit.
MARION. (*Sits on the edge of the examining table while Sgt. Thech checks him for reflexes.*) You're terrific you are! You and Pegeen ought to team up. She was my first wife. Talk about your lady wrestlers and roller-derby queens! But next to you, she was Snow White. But I foxed her. Just when she thought she had me where she wanted me, I sprang the divorce on her. On what grounds, may I ask? she growled . . . fat hands on her fat hips . . . Dutch Cleanser I used to call her. On exactly what grounds? (*Sgt. Thech is busy completing some forms.*) Mental cruelty, I smiled, and boy did that answer ever throw her for a loop! She begged me to change it to adultery but I held firm. You should have seen the look on that judge's face in Juarez when I dropped that little bombshell. Mental cruelty!
SGT. THECH. All right, Mr. Cheever, you can get dressed now. Your physical examination is over.
MARION. (*Caught in midair.*) Oh. It's over. Well that wasn't so bad. How did I do? Am I 4-F?
SGT. THECH. You have nothing to worry about. I found no evidence of physical abnormality.
MARION. (*Aghast.*) You found no evidence of physical abnormality? Now wait a minute. What about my labile blood presure? Oh no, sergeant, I'm not done in here. Not yet. I want more testing. You're not convinced. I'm not leaving until I get a better verdict. What about my sinus condition? Did you know I had one? Of course not, you didn't look up my nose. What kind of examination is it without looking up a person's nose? A lot of things could be wrong up there. I can't breathe seven months out of the year. Would you write that down, please? And what about my eye test? I know I failed my eye test!
SGT. THECH. (*Busy at her desk tabulating the examination results.*) If you won't cooperate, I have to judge you on the basis of objective evidence. You do not squint, you do not wear glasses and you saw my lips moving at a distance of over fifteen feet away. We have ways of evaluating the condition of a subject whether the

subject cooperates or not. You'd have to be a lot smarter and better rehearsed than you are to fool an examining officer.

MARION. (*Triumphant.*) All right, then what about my feet? You didn't even make me take my socks off. That's all right, I'll do it myself. Here. Now look at this. They're flat. I'm not ashamed. See how flat they are? Do you see any arch? Of course you don't. You call that normal? And see, see all those corns? My feet are covered with corns. And I'll tell you something, something highly abnormal: I was born with all these corns. That's right, sergeant, I was born with corns. They are hereditary. Ask yourself, is that normal? (*Sgt. Thech continues working at desk.*) And look! (*He shakes his arms in front of her.*) No muscle tone. All flab! See how the skin just hangs there? And it's not a question of diet. I've dieted all my life. I simply don't burn fat! (*Now showing her his teeth.*) And teeth! My teeth. They're full of decay. If I have a candy bar I have to have an inlay. I swear to God I do. My gums are very spongy. I mean I'll probably have a coronary in five years . . . if I live very carefully. (*Desperately trying to attract Sgt. Thech's attention.*) And sergeant, here, watch this, look now, sergeant, over here, see this? . . . (*He removes his toupee.*) You didn't know that, did you? It fools lots of people but there it is. I lost all of my hair in a period of thirteen months after my last divorce. It just went! Right out by the roots it came. Is that normal to lose so much hair in thirteen months? And that's not hereditary, sergeant. My father still has every hair in his head. You know what my kind of hair loss is? Nerves, sergeant, plain old-fashioned nerves! It's highly irregular he should have all his and I don't have mine! And what about my mind? You haven't asked me one single question about my mind. For all you know I could be a raving lunatic. I could be a—

SGT. THECH. (*She's into the psychological and intelligence tests.*) I have twelve apples.

MARION. (*Thrown.*) You have what?

SGT. THECH. You have twelve apples. Together we have . . .

MARION. (*Involuntarily.*) Twenty-four apples. (*He realizes what he's done and groans.*)

SGT. THECH. I have a pie which I wish to divide as follows: one-fourth of the pie to Fred, one-fourth of the pie to Phyllis, one-fourth of the pie to you. How much pie will I have left for myself?

MARION. (*Thinks a moment.*) Who are Fred and Phyllis? I

mean maybe Phyllis didn't finish all her piece and then there'd be more for you. A quarter and a half!

SGT. THECH. You are on a train going sixty miles an hour. Your destination is a hundred and twenty away. How many hours will it take you to get to your destination?

MARION. I would say three days. But then I don't take trains. I really wouldn't swear to that answer.

SGT. THECH. Who was the first President of the United States?

MARION. George Washington. Was that right?

SGT. THECH. Who were the allies of the United States in the Second World War?

MARION. The good people.

SGT. THECH. Who were its enemies?

MARION. No one. We had no enemies.

SGT. THECH. Who are the allies of the United States now?

MARION. Just about everyone.

SGT. THECH. Who are its enemies?

MARION. Who can tell?

SGT. THECH. Name three of the twelve Apostles.

MARION. Joseph . . . and his brother . . . and his sister!

SGT. THECH. In what year did Columbus discover America?

MARION. 1776. No, wait, it was 1775!

SGT. THECH. What is the great pox and how does it differ from the small pox?

MARION. The great pox is greater than the small pox. However, both are poxes.

SGT. THECH. If you found an unopened letter lying on the sidewalk, fully addressed and stamped, what would you do?

MARION. I would probably step on it. I mean who wouldn't? You're walking along, you'd be surprised what you step on.

SGT. THECH. If you were seated in a theatre and you saw a fire break out nearby before the rest of the audience noticed it—what would you do?

MARION. This one's right up my alley. As a theatre manager I know about this. The main thing is I wouldn't want to start a panic. So I'd very quietly leave and go home.

SGT. THECH. If you found a wallet lying on the sidewalk—what would you do?

MARION. I'd be delighted. I never find anything.

SGT. THECH. What is the similarity between a chair and a couch?
MARION. A chair and a couch? You can sit on them.
SGT. THECH. A rabbit and a squirrel.
MARION. (*Reasonably.*) You could sit on a rabbit and a squirrel. The rabbit might even like it.
SGT. THECH. What is the difference between a giant and a dwarf.
MARION. The difference? I see the similarity all right but the difference is tricky.
SGT. THECH. A profit and a loss.
MARION. A profit is when the loss is greater than the sum. It's exactly like giants and drawfs.
SGT. THECH. A man and a gorilla.
MARION. Hair. Lots of hair.
SGT. THECH. Complete the following sentences. People obey the law because . . .
MARION. Because! Because they have to obey it.
SGT. THECH. I am happiest when my family is . . .
MARION. Yes! I think we all are. Well, aren't you?
SGT. THECH. What is the meaning of the following proverbs. He who laughs last laughs best.
MARION. Yes . . . well . . . that means that *he* who laughs *last* laughs *best.*
SGT. THECH. A rolling stone gathers no moss.
MARION. That's one of my favorites. It means that a rolling *stone* . . . gathers no *moss!*
SGT. THECH. I am going to say a word.
MARION. Did I get that one right?
SGT. THECH. After I say it I want you to say the first word that comes to your mind without thinking.
MARION. Are you sure?
SGT. THECH. You have one second. Tree. Tree!
MARION. I'm sorry. I was thinking. I couldn't help myself.
SGT. THECH. House.
MARION. House. The first word that comes to mind when you say house is house.
SGT. THECH. Father.
MARION. (*Drawing a blank.*) Father . . . father . . .
SGT. THECH. Grass.

MARION. Green. There, I got one!
SGT. THECH. Shower.
MARION. Tree. When it showers you stand under a tree with your father.
SGT. THECH. Snake.
MARION. Juicy. Juicy snake.
SGT. THECH. House.
MARION. Whores. No, no! that's not right.
SGT. THECH. Mother.
MARION. None. I mean—
SGT. THECH. Green.
MARION. Colors. Green colors.
SGT. THECH. Floor.
MARION. Me. Really! I'm on my feet all day.
SGT. THECH. Purse.
MARION. Snatch. Purse snatcher.
SGT. THECH. Have you ever suffered from night terrors?
MARION. Terribly.
SGT. THECH. Insomnia.
MARION. Of course insomnia! Because of the night terrors.
SGT. THECH. Sleepwalking.
MARION. Absolutely! In the morning my ankles are so swollen!
SGT. THECH. Anxiety states.
MARION. This is so good in here this part! Keep on.
SGT. THECH. Hallucinations.
MARION. Of grandeur. Of course terrible grandeur!
SGT. THECH. Delusions.
MARION. They're not the same thing? Listen, can't we go back to the anxiety states?
SGT. THECH. Compulsive eating.
MARION. No, I've never been bothered by that. About my anxiety states—!
SGT. THECH. Have you ever indulged in homosexual activities.
MARION. They have been very good to me.
SGT. THECH. When did you stop?
MARION. Who said anything about stopping? They're a small but vital minority. The Fine Arts Theatre welcomes them.
SGT. THECH. Did you have a normal relationship with your mother?
MARION. I'm sure she thought so!

SGT. THECH. Did you have a normal relationship with your father?

MARION. After we stopped dating the same girl, everything was fine.

SGT. THECH. Do you have any history of bedwetting?

MARION. Even my top sheet is rubber.

SGT. THECH. Have you ever attempted suicide?

MARION. No, but I've thought of murder.

SGT. THECH. Are you now or have you ever been a member of the Communist party?

MARION. I wouldn't be surprised. I mean you join anything nowadays and next thing you know it's pinko.

SGT. THECH. What is your responsibility to your community.

MARION. Unh . . . to shovel the snow.

SGT. THECH. What is your responsibility to your family.

MARION. To be there.

SGT. THECH. What is your responsibility to your country.

MARION. To be there.

SGT. THECH. (*Abruptly.*) All right, Mr. Cheever, you may go now. The examination is over.

MARION. The whole thing?

SGT. THECH. That's right.

MARION. Well? How did I do? Am I 4-F yet?

SGT. THECH. I don't think you have anything to worry about. I doubt if they would find someone like you acceptable.

MARION. (*Stung, but hiding it.*) Oh well good. Good. Based on what? The last two answers?

SGT. THECH. The entire psychological examination.

MARION. I see. Well, then I *am* 4-F?

SGT. THECH. You'll get your classification in the mail.

MARION. I can hardly wait.

SGT. THECH. You may go now. I'm through with you. (*Sgt. Thech turns her back to him and begins typing up his test results.*)

MARION. (*Beginning to dress.*) Oh don't worry, I'm going. Nothing in the world could make me stay here. Granted, I've enjoyed all this. I mean you've been just wonderful. It must be difficult examining someone while they're still alive and breathing! And your attention has been so flattering. I'm not used to so much fuss. You're great, just great. The way you concentrated on me. I never distracted you from me once. I'm sure you have a big future ahead of you. (*Sgt. Thech types.*) Now you're through with me and would like me to go. You have taken my time, you have taken my blood, you have taken my urine, you have taken secrets and now you would like me out of here so you can digest them in private. Isn't that right? Well I'm not going. If I go I take *all* of me with me. I'd like my blood and my urine back! I mean I'm 4-F, you can't have any use for them. (*Sgt. Thech types.*) You know I am not simply the sum total of my parts. I am someone. I am a citizen. I have my rights. I pay my taxes, I serve my jury duty, I buy American. I don't make trouble. I support the administration. I keep my mouth shut. I believe everything I read. I do all that and that gives me rights! I want my blood and my urine back and I . . . I demand an apology! I have given everything to everyone and now I want something back! Don't tell me about responsibilities. I visit my kids, I bring them presents; I visit my father, I bring him presents; I visit my sisters, their kids get presents, too. I pay my rent; I pay my alimony; I meet my car payments—a hot red Mustang I can hardly fit behind the wheel of, but I'm meeting those payments! I do everything I'm supposed to do . . . I'm never late for work . . . and now I demand a reward! I want a reward. You owe me something. My country owes me something. Somebody owes me something. Because I have nothing! My big break? A lousy twenty-bucks raise. Big deal, crap! My children don't give a damn. What do I get on Father's Day? A lot of crap from Woolworth's their mothers picked out. My father doesn't recognize my voice on the telephone. My mother is dead. I've been married twice. You think it's fun, a man my age going home alone at night? Who looks at men like me after a while? I know what I look like! I'm no fool! (*Sgt. Thech continues typing.*) You know what the ushers at the theatre call me behind my back? Fatso. Yeah! that hurts. But when I become *the* manager I am going to fire those ushers and hire new ushers and *they* will call me Fatso behind my back. Because that is exactly what I am. A fatso. I am nothing but what I eat. But I feed myself. Nobody feeds me. And I eat everything I want. When I want candy, I eat candy. When I want a pizza at two A.M., I call up and order pizza. I'm going to get older and fatter and someday I'm going to die from overweight and smoking. But when I go, I'm paying for my own funeral and I'm going to give myself the best funeral that money can buy. Because dead or alive

I pay my own way! Those niggers on relief, can they say that? They cannot! And they get to do everything. They get to riot, they get to loot, they get to yell, they get to hate, they get to kill! They get in the papers, they get on television and everybody pays attention. Everybody cares. And what do I get? There's nothing on television about me. My name's not in the Sunday papers. And I'm the one who does everything he should. I'm the one who never makes trouble. I'm the good citizen. But everybody else gets to do everything! You see those teen-age girls with their skirts up to here strutting around with their hair all piled up and driving a man crazy. And those men all like fags with that hair and those pants. They do anything they want. They have anything they want. And I get shit! (*He bangs on Sgt. Thech's desk with his fist. Sgt. Thech goes on typing.*) How dare you call me in here, examine me, ignore me, dismiss me and tell me I'm not acceptable! *You* are not acceptable! I want my orange juice. You took my blood and I want my orange juice. I know my rights. I want my radiator fixed. I want those people next door to turn their radio down when I bang on the wall. I want quiet. I want my sleep. I want them to stop all those parties upstairs. I want people to listen to me when I call up and make complaints. Not just sit there and type. Stop it! And listen to me! (*Sgt. Thech has finished typing up her report.*) I said stop! (*He puts his hands over the typewriter keys.*) Good. Very good! (*Now Marion will describe everything Sgt. Thech does while she is doing it—as if he were giving her the orders to do it.*) That's right. Fold the paper. Open the drawer. Put it away. Close it. Now you're doing exactly as you're told. Get up. Fold the sheet. Check the instruments. Make sure you've got everything. One final check now. Excellent. Now out you go. Close the door. There! (*Sgt. Thech has left the room, closing the door behind her.*) All right, on the scale now, Cheever! Do I have to? Why not? There's nothing to be afraid of. (*Marion gets on the scale.*) You're the perfect weight, just right for your height. You're an excellent physical specimen, Cheever. Am I? You're in very good shape. You're very acceptable. (*Marion steps off the scale.*) On the table now. (*Marion crosses to the examination table.*) Lie down. (*Marion obeys.*) Give me your arm. Will it hurt? Not you, Cheever. You're very brave. (*Marion moves his lips silently: "Can you hear what I'm saying?"*) Yes, you said, "Can you hear what I'm saying?" Your hearing is perfect. I know. Now read the chart. The last line, the smallest letters. "A-W-G-H-L." Excellent, you have perfect vision. Rest now. Thank you. (*Marion lets his head drop on the table.*) Tell me about it. I was thirteen years old. Yes, go on. I came home and she wasn't there. Yes. It was so sudden. None of us knew. We all thought she would always be there and then when she wasn't . . . (*His voice trails off in tears.*) You must have been very sad. I was, I was. I felt so cold. Didn't you tell anyone how you felt? Nobody asked me. I'm asking you. I never got to say good-bye. I understand. (*Short pause.*) On your feet now. I don't think I can. Yes, Cheever, you can do it. You're very strong now and very brave and very acceptable. (*Marion gets up off the table.*) Up now, shoulders back, walk tall. That's it. You're doing fine. (*Marion goes to Sgt. Thech's desk, puts on her white examination coat which she has left over her chair, sits, types a moment, then looks up.*) You have ten seconds to strip. By the power vested in me by the United States government I order you to remove all articles of clothing. One one-thousand, two one-thousand, three one-thousand, four one-thousand. Sorry. You are not acceptable. (*His head spins around as he looks straight ahead into the audience.*) NEXT! (*The lights snap off.*)

CURTAIN

PROPERTY PLOT

On Stage:

- Examination table
- Scale (upright)
- Cabinet with medical equipment:
  - Stethoscope
  - Tongue depressor
  - Small medical flashlight
  - Eye chart
  - Blood pressure kit
  - Syringe
  - Test tube
- Desk, with:
  - Typewriter
  - Papers and forms
  - Pen
- 2 chairs
- American flag, on stand
- Sheet
- Sink
- Towel

Off Stage:

- MARION:
  - Briefcase, with:
    - Card
    - Bottle with "urine specimen"
  - Cigarette case and lighter

- SGT. THECH:
  - White medical coat

BOTTICELLI

by

Terrence McNally

BOTTICELLI was first produced by Channel 13 in New York City on March 14 and 15, 1968. The cast included Kevin O'Connor and Roy London. The director was Glen Jordan.

CHARACTERS

WAYNE

STU

MAN

If the play is produced in an arena-type theatre, I would suggest the Man make his appearance through the audience. In a proscenium theatre, he might make his way down the center aisle with a follow spot on him. He must be center stage at the end of the play, a single light on his face.

BOTTICELLI

Jungle foliage. Afternoon sun and shadows. Insect noises. Two soldiers, Wayne and Stu, crouching with rifles.

WAYNE. No, I'm not Marcel Proust.
STU. Proust was a stylist.
WAYNE. And he died *after* World War I.
STU. You sure?
WAYNE. 1922.
STU. Yeah?
WAYNE. November 4, 19—
STU. All right! (*Then.*) What's up?
WAYNE. (*Stiffening.*) I thought I heard something. (*Relaxes.*)
STU. Are you a . . . let's see . . . are you a Polish concert pianist who donated a large part of the proceeds from his concerts to the cause of Polish nationalism?
WAYNE. Oh that's a real brain-crusher, that one is!
STU. Well are you?
WAYNE. No I'm not Paderewski.
STU. Are you sure you're dead?
WAYNE. Oh brother!
STU. A dead European male in the arts beginning with "P"?
WAYNE. Why don't you write it down?
STU. Got it! You're a controversial Russian poet, novelist, dramatist and short story writer.
WAYNE. Sorry. I'm not Pushkin.
STU. Pushkin wasn't considered controversial.
WAYNE. Who says?
STU. I do.
WAYNE. He was part Negro.
STU. What's controversial about that?
WAYNE. Dumas *père?*
STU. Don't change the subject. Controversial Russian writer. Come on. I've got you stumped, hunh? Look at you. Drew a blank. Hunh? Hunh?

WAYNE. I hope it's not Boris Pasternak you're crowing about.
STU. Drop dead, will you?
WAYNE. Then give up, hunh? (*Tenses.*) Sshh! (*Relaxes.*) Not yet.
STU. You'd think he'd starve in there by now.
WAYNE. Maybe he has. Why don't you go see?
STU. And get a grenade in the face. That tunnel could be half a mile long for all we know. He's buried in there like a groundhog. No, sir, I'm holding tight, staying right where I am, sergeant's orders. I got all the time in the world to wait for that bugger to stick his head out. (*Wayne starts making cigarette.*) Are you a . . . ? I'm running dry. P's the hardest letter in the alphabet.
WAYNE. Wanna turn on?
STU. How much we got left?
WAYNE. If he's not out of there by tonight we're in trouble.
STU. Do you keep a diary?
WAYNE. Sure. Every night.
STU. No, who you are! Does he keep a diary?
WAYNE. I'm not Samuel Pepys.
STU. Smart ass! (*They smoke.*) Would you say this is the best part of the whole war?
WAYNE. What is?
STU. This. Pot.
WAYNE. No. I'd say Raquel Welch.
STU. Yeah.
WAYNE. What'd you think of her?
STU. I didn't.
WAYNE. Those goddam white leather boots up to here . . . and that yellow miniskirt . . .
STU. Hey, are you the outstanding English Baroque composer?
WAYNE. I'm not Henry Purcell. I thought Raquel Welch looked like a sexy . . . ostrich.
STU. Do the words "Rape of the Lock" mean anything to you?
WAYNE. No, and they don't mean anything to Alexander Pope either.
STU. Nuts!
WAYNE. Look, let me tell you who I am, hunh?
STU. No I said.
WAYNE. Brother, you're stubborn.

STU. And *you're* a Victorian playwright!
WAYNE. I'm not Arthur Wing Pinero.
STU. Sir.
WAYNE. Hunh?
STU. Sir Arthur Wing Pinero.
WAYNE. I know!
STU. You didn't say it.
WAYNE. I'd rather talk about Raquel Welch.
STU. Sure you would. You're getting stoned.
WAYNE. I'm not getting anything else.
STU. You still worrying about that letter from Susan?
WAYNE. Not since Raquel Welch I'm not.
STU. I bet.
WAYNE. Let her get a divorce. I don't care. Hell, the only mistake I made was thinking I had to marry her. I should've sent her to Puerto Rico. She couldn've had a vacation on me, too.
STU. Only you had scruples.
WAYNE. Leave me alone.
STU. Jesuit high school, Dominican college scruples.
WAYNE. God, you're insensitive. Wait'll *you* get married.
STU. Maybe I never will.
WAYNE. Yeah!
STU. I might not.
WAYNE. You'd marry the first girl who looked twice at you. Yours is one wedding I wouldn't want to miss. There's always Marlene Schroll.
STU. As You Desire Me!
WAYNE. What the—?
STU. You wrote As You Desire Me.
WAYNE. I'm not Luigi Pirandello.
STU. Okay, but simmer down, hunh?
WAYNE. It's a dumb game.
STU. Your idea.
WAYNE. I was trying to kill time.
STU. Well if we had something intelligent to discuss . . .
WAYNE. What's wrong with Raquel Welch?
STU. Nothing. She's the quintessence of intelligence.
WAYNE. I'm gonna bust you in the mouth. (*Pause.*) I wish I'd burned my draft card.
STU. Are you a Russian composer?

WAYNE. I'm not Prokofiev.
STU. An Italian composer?
WAYNE. I'm not Puccini.
STU. An Italian composer?
WAYNE. I'm not Ponchielli.
STU. An Italian composer?
WAYNE. What are you, a record?
STU. An Italian composer?
WAYNE. All right, who?
STU. Pizzarella.
WAYNE. Go to hell.
STU. What's wrong with Pizzarella?
WAYNE. There's no Italian composer named Pizzarella.
STU. How do you know?
WAYNE. I know!
STU. Well maybe there is.
WAYNE. Yeah and you just made him up. Pizzarella. Look, if you're gonna play, play fair. Boy, you haven't changed since college. Even in charades you'd try to put something over.
STU. Like when?
WAYNE. Like when you did "The Brothers Karamazov." Only you did it in Russian. How could anybody guess the "Brothers Karamazov" in a game of charades when *you* were doing it in Russian?
STU. It would've been too easy in English.
WAYNE. No wonder you never made the chess and bridge teams. Those are precise games. You don't muck with the rules in *them*. (*Pause.*) Typical. Sulk now.
STU. I'm thinking.
WAYNE. (*Rolls over on back, looks up at sky.*) You know what I can't get over?
STU. Mmmmmm.
WAYNE. Poor Father Reilly.
STU. Yeah.
WAYNE. I mean just dropping dead like that. God, we were lucky having him for a teacher. And of all places to drop dead. He loved Rome the same way some men love women. I think he lived for his summer vacations. As much as he gave his students, his heart was always in Rome on the Spanish Steps or the Pincio.

And I guess it was all those steps and hills that finally killed him. A great man.

STU. Wayne?

WAYNE. Yeah?

STU. An Italian composer?

WAYNE. You see this fist?

STU. I just thought of two more.

WAYNE. Real ones?

STU. Give up, you'll see.

WAYNE. If they're not, buddy . . . !

STU. (*Looking at watch.*) You've got fifteen seconds.

WAYNE. Unh . . . unh . . . unh . . . quit making me nervous . . . unh . . .

STU. Ten!

WAYNE. Palestrina!

STU. Who else?

WAYNE. Palestrina and . . . unh . . .

STU. Pizzarella?

WAYNE. Can it! Palestrina and . . .

STU. Five seconds.

WAYNE. Pergolesi. Giovanni Pergolesi! (*Burst of machine gun fire, they both flatten out.*) That dirty little . . . (*Aims, ready to fire.*)

STU. (*Terse whisper.*) Homosexual Greek philosopher.

WAYNE. Brother, are you warped. I mean that's disgusting.

STU. Come on.

WAYNE. Plato wasn't homosexual.

STU. You were right there, climbing the Acropolis.

WAYNE. Your mind is really sick. A remark like that turns my stomach.

STU. Who made any remarks?

WAYNE. It's not even funny. (*Firing stops.*) Where the hell is he? Come on, buster, stick your neck out. He's shooting to see if anybody's out here. We'll just have to sit tight.

STU. Apropos the Parthenon, did you by any chance supervise the re-building of it?

WAYNE. I'm not Phidias. What are we on now? Your Greek kick?

STU. You're a fine one to talk about *that*.

WAYNE. There's something crawling on you.

STU. Hey! What the hell is it? This country. Bugs in your shoes, bugs in your hair, bugs in your food. Look at him go. Eight legs . . . no, ten! . . . I guess those are wings . . . nice antennae . . . I used to be scared of bugs.
WAYNE. Do you have to have a conversation with him?
STU. Bonsoir, bug. (*Crushes bug.*)
WAYNE. I could never do that.
STU. Bugs have souls now, too?
WAYNE. Shut up about all that, will you?
STU. I don't suppose you're an Italian poet?
WAYNE. I'm not Petrarch, Einstein.
STU. It was just a wild guess.
WAYNE. You're never going to get me.
STU. I'm not going to give up either.
WAYNE. Stubborn, stubborn, stubborn!
STU. I'd lose all self-respect if I weren't.
WAYNE. Sshh.
STU. I mean the only reason to begin a game is to win it.
WAYNE. I said shut up! (*The Man has come out of the tunnel. He's young, emaciated. He pauses at the entrance, quivering like a frightened rabbit. Spot on him.*) Look at the little bugger.
STU. Not so little through these sights.
WAYNE. Not yet! He has to come this way. Wait'll he's closer.
STU. You're not a French painter? A great master of the classical school?
WAYNE. I'm not Poussin.
STU. I've got another one. Impressionist.
WAYNE. French.
STU. Yeah.
WAYNE. I'm not Pisaro.
STU. I can't think of any more P's.
WAYNE. All right, *you* gave up, I'm—
STU. No! (*Man has begun to move cautiously away from tunnel opening.*)
WAYNE. Here he comes. Quiet now.
STU. Were you an Italian sculptor working with Giotto on the campanile in Florence.
WAYNE. I'm not Pisano. Get ready.
STU. Okay, and this is it, Wayne. Did you write a famous "Lives"?

WAYNE. I'm not Plutarch. Let's go. (*Man's face contorts with pain as he is cut down by a seemingly endless volley of gunfire. He falls, twitches, finally lies still. Wayne and Stu approach.*)
STU. Is he dead? I just asked!
WAYNE. Let's get back to camp.
STU. Okay, I give up. Who are you?
WAYNE. Pollaiuolo.
STU. Who?
WAYNE. Pollaiuolo. Antonio del Pollaiuolo.
STU. That's like Pizzarella. (*They start moving off. Spot stays on Man's face.*)
WAYNE. Italian painter, sculptor and goldsmith. 1432–1498.
STU. Well I never heard of him.
WAYNE. Famous for his landscapes and the movement he put into the human body.
STU. Never heard of him.
WAYNE. He influenced Dürer, Signorelli and Verrocchio. (*They are just voices now.*)
STU. *Them* I've heard of.
WAYNE. Portrait of a Man? The Labors of Hercules? David? The Martyrdom of St. Sebastian? Tobias and the Angel?
STU. Never heard of him.
WAYNE. The tomb of Sixtus IV?
STU. Never heard of him.
WAYNE. Good God, he was a contemporary of Botticelli!
STU. Never heard of him.
WAYNE. Christ, you're dumb.
STU. I NEVER HEARD OF HIM. (*Spot stays on Man's face. Slow fade.*)

PROPERTY PLOT

Rifles (2)

Helmets (2)

Marijuana

Cigarette paper

Watch (Stu)